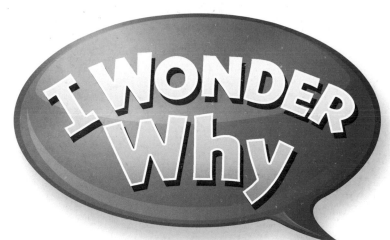

I WONDER Why

Kangaroos Have Pouches

and other questions about baby animals

Jenny Wood

KINGFISHER
NEW YORK

Copyright © 2011 by Kingfisher
Published in the United States by Kingfisher,
175 Fifth Ave., New York, NY 10010
Kingfisher is an imprint of Macmillan Children's Books, London.
All rights reserved.

First published 1995 by Kingfisher
This edition published 2011 by Kingfisher

Distributed in the U.S. and Canada by Macmillan,
175 Fifth Ave., New York, NY 10010

LIBRARY OF CONGRESS CATALOGING-IN-PUBLICATION DATA
has been applied for.

ISBN 978-0-7534-6559-2 (HC)
ISBN 978-0-7534-6528-8 (PB)

Kingfisher books are available for special promotions and
premiums. For details contact: Special Markets Department,
Macmillan, 175 Fifth Ave., New York, NY 10010.

For more information, please visit www.kingfisherbooks.com

Printed in China
9 8 7 6 5 4 3 2
2TR/0512/UTD/WKT/140MA

Consultant: Michael Chinery
Illustrations: John Butler 18–19; Joanne Cowne 14–15, 24–25;
Peter Dennis (Linda Rogers) 26–27; Chris Forsey 16–17, 28–29;
Tony Kenyon (B.L. Kearley) all cartoons; Mick Loates (Linden
Artists) 6–7; Alan Male (Linden Artists) 10–11; Nicki Palin 4–5,
30–31; Andrea Ricciardi di Gaudesi 22–23; Claudia Saraceni
8–9; Dan Wright 20–21; David Wright (Kathy Jakeman)
cover, 12–13.

CONTENTS

Which baby has the best mother?

A baby gorilla has one of the best moms in the world. A grownup gorilla may look a little scary to us, but she's loving and gentle to her young. As well as grooming the baby, she feeds it for up to three years and protects and helps it for even longer.

Gorillas are a type of ape—along with chimpanzees, gibbons, and orangutans. All apes make very good mothers.

Which baby has the worst mother?

The female European cuckoo can't be bothered to take care of her chicks. This lazy mom lays an egg in another bird's nest. When the egg hatches, it's the other bird that does all the hard work raising the chick.

The cuckoo manages to trick birds because her egg matches the other ones in the nest.

Which mother has her babies in jail?

While the female hornbill lays her eggs in a hole in a tree, the male helps her block up the door. But he leaves a hole for her beak so that he can feed her while she's stuck inside!

Tree shrews are part-time moms. They leave their babies in the nest, stopping by to feed them only every other day.

Which father gives birth to his young?

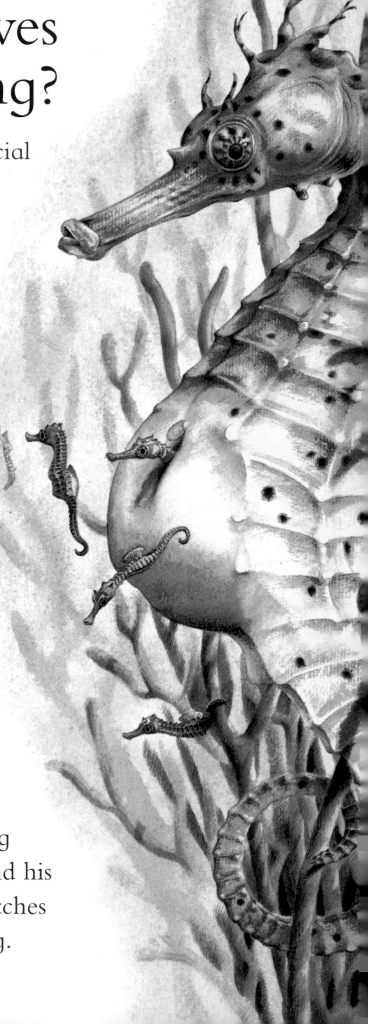

The male sea horse has a special pouch on his body where the female lays her eggs. The male has to carry them around until they hatch, and then hundreds of baby sea horses shoot out into the water.

Whose feet keep an egg warm?

Every year, in the middle of the winter, a female emperor penguin lays one egg and gives it to her mate to keep warm. He balances the egg between his feet and his feathers until it hatches in the early spring.

Male sticklebacks care for their young. If a baby tries to swim away, the dad grabs it in his mouth and spits it back into the nest.

Which father has a chest like a sponge?

Sand grouse live in the dry desert areas of Africa, Asia, and southern Europe. When water's in short supply, the male flies hundreds of miles to a watering hole and soaks up water in his feathers. Then he flies back to his thirsty chicks and lets them suck out the water for a long, refreshing drink.

Many animal fathers play no part in bringing up their young. Most of them leave before the babies are even born.

Why do kangaroos have pouches?

Only female kangaroos have a pouch. The males don't have babies, so they don't need one!

A pouch is a safe place for a baby to grow. A newborn kangaroo is only the size of a peanut. It struggles through its mom's fur until it reaches her warm pouch. There, it feeds on her milk and continues growing.

Who clings on for dear life?

A baby lemur rides on its mom's back for the first seven months of its life. It wraps its legs around her and holds on tightly as she leaps through the forest on a hair-raising ride.

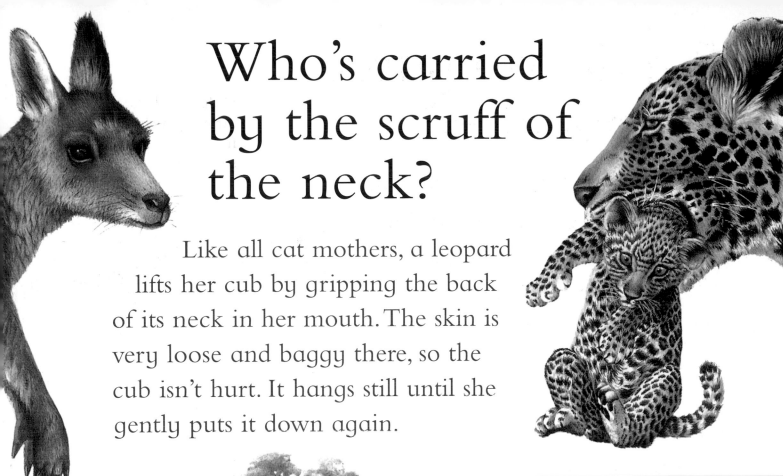

Who's carried by the scruff of the neck?

Like all cat mothers, a leopard lifts her cub by gripping the back of its neck in her mouth. The skin is very loose and baggy there, so the cub isn't hurt. It hangs still until she gently puts it down again.

A female crocodile carries her babies in her mouth, being careful not to bite them with her razor-sharp teeth.

Who likes a ride on the water?

Baby grebes often ride along on their mother's back. But they don't have to. They're perfectly able to swim on their own!

Which baby has lots of aunts?

As well as having a mother, a baby elephant has lots of aunts. That's because female elephants live in large family groups of up to 50 animals. In fact, a new calf not only has plenty of aunts but also has grandmothers, sisters, and cousins, too!

Which babies live in a nursery?

Mara parents leave their babies under the ground. To make sure they're not lonely, many families share the same burrow. When a mother stops by to feed her young, she checks on the other mara babies, too.

When a hippo mother goes away to feed, she leaves her calf with a babysitter!

Maras live in South America. They're a kind of long-legged guinea pig. Mara parents never join their babies in the burrow. They whistle down the hole, and the young come scampering out!

Which is the biggest nursery?

Bracken Cave in Texas is home to more than 20 million bats. The mothers leave their babies in a nursery, huddled together for warmth. The bats are so tightly packed that there may be 1,000 in a space the size of a doormat.

Bees use nurseries, too. The eggs hatch in a special part of the hive.

A bat mother has such sharp hearing that she can recognize her baby's call out of millions of others in the cave.

What's inside a bird's egg?

There are three things inside a bird's egg—a baby bird, a yellow yolk, and a clear jelly called the white. The yolk is food for the growing bird. The white is food, too, but it also protects the bird if the egg gets knocked.

Some eggs don't get the chance to hatch. They are eaten by hungry hunters.

Some eggs hatch quickly, while others hatch more slowly. A baby housefly hatches in 24 hours. But a kiwi chick takes three months or longer.

Whale sharks lay the biggest eggs—they're the size of a football.

Why do birds turn their eggs?

Birds turn their eggs so that every part of each egg gets its fair share of warmth. Baby birds need warmth to grow—that's why a parent has to sit on the nest.

Is it only birds that lay eggs?

Fish, frogs, snakes, turtles, insects, and spiders—all sorts of animals lay eggs. The eggs look and feel different. Turtle eggs are soft and leathery and are the size of golf balls. Butterfly eggs are tiny and often sparkle like shiny jewels.

Caterpillars must be born hungry. Many of them gobble up their eggshells as they hatch.

13

Which baby has the comfiest nest?

Baby rabbits live in a nest that is very cozy. Their mother builds it inside a burrow, plumping dry grass stalks into a cushion and then covering it with her own soft fur.

Who is born under the snow?

Polar bear cubs are born in an underground den that their mother digs deep in the snow. Warm air is trapped inside the den, making it a surprisingly snug place to spend the winter months.

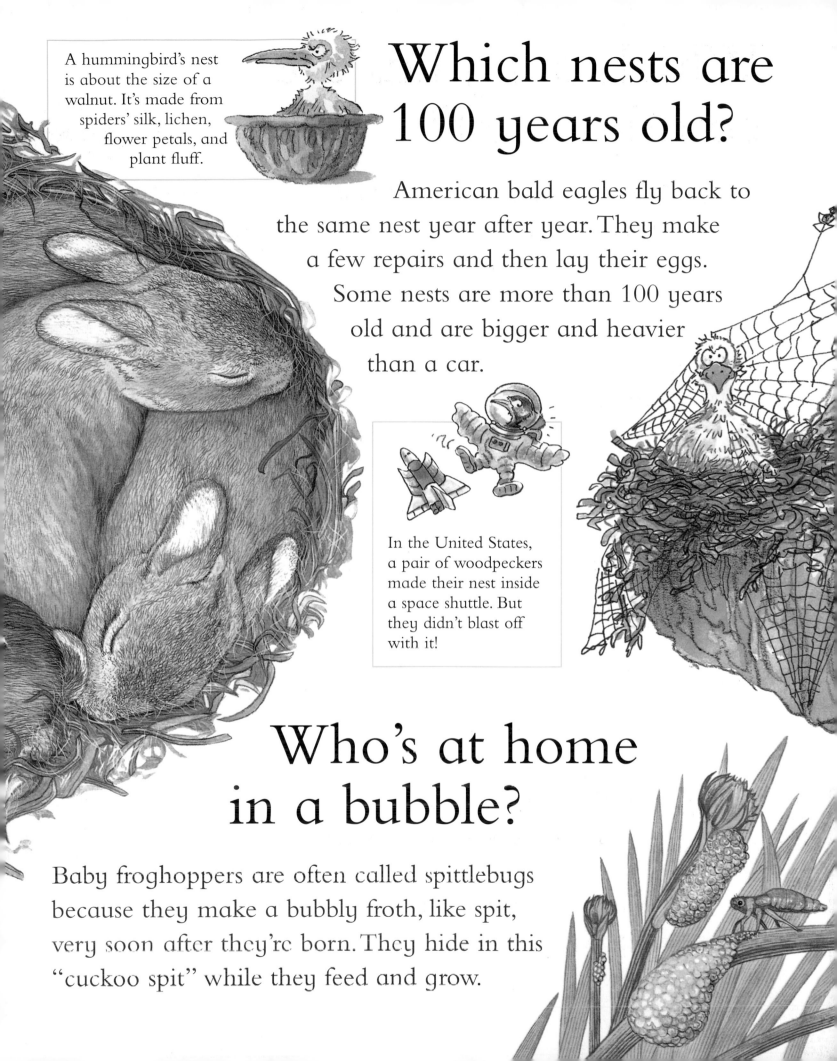

A hummingbird's nest is about the size of a walnut. It's made from spiders' silk, lichen, flower petals, and plant fluff.

Which nests are 100 years old?

American bald eagles fly back to the same nest year after year. They make a few repairs and then lay their eggs. Some nests are more than 100 years old and are bigger and heavier than a car.

In the United States, a pair of woodpeckers made their nest inside a space shuttle. But they didn't blast off with it!

Who's at home in a bubble?

Baby froghoppers are often called spittlebugs because they make a bubbly froth, like spit, very soon after they're born. They hide in this "cuckoo spit" while they feed and grow.

Which is the biggest baby in the world?

The baby blue whale is a real whopper, weighing up to 6,600 pounds (3,000kg)—that's as much as 1,000 human babies! As soon as it is born, its mom nudges it to the surface to take its first breath of air.

A baby blue whale is as long as five scuba divers swimming head to toe.

The baby howler monkey is a champion screamer. Its cries can be heard even through thick rainforest.

Which is the tallest baby?

A baby giraffe is about 6 feet (2m) tall—that's taller than most grown-up people. The mother giraffe is even taller and gives birth standing up. Her new baby hits the ground feet first. Ouch! It's a long way to fall.

Which is the ugliest baby?

One of the ugliest-looking babies is the vulture chick, with its big hooked beak and bare head and neck. But then its parents aren't very beautiful, either.

17

Why do pandas have one baby at a time?

A mother giant panda gives her cub so much love and attention that she can cope with only one at a time. By caring for her cub for a year or more, she is helping make sure that her baby survives.

There aren't many pandas left. Zookeepers fly their pandas around the world so that they can meet other pandas—and hopefully have babies.

Which animals lay hundreds of eggs?

Most frogs and toads lay hundreds of eggs in a big frothy mass called spawn. Many of the eggs are eaten, but some survive and hatch into tadpoles.

The giant clam may have the biggest family of all. Every year, the female lays a huge cloud of eggs—at least a billion of them!

Which family is always identical?

Each time a nine-banded armadillo gives birth, she has four identical babies. They are either all female or all male. This is because a single egg inside the mother splits into four, and all four parts begin to grow— into identical quadruplets!

Albatross moms lay only one egg every two years. The chick is cared for by its parents for about ten months, until it's big enough to fly.

Which baby drinks the creamiest milk?

A seal pup has to grow quickly so that its mother can go off and catch fish. She spends three weeks just feeding her pup— after that, she's starving!

A mother harp seal's milk is so thick and rich that it looks more like mayonnaise than milk. It's about 12 times creamier than cow's milk and is such good food that you can almost see a harp seal pup growing fatter as it feeds!

Many seal pups are born in the coldest parts of the world. But they don't freeze to death because they have a thick layer of fat covered by a furry coat to keep them nice and warm.

20

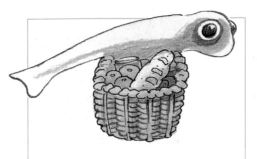

A baby salmon hatches with its own ready-made lunch! The tiny fish has a pouch of food, rather like an egg yolk, that keeps it going for several weeks.

Which parent serves meals in a bag?

The pelican has a baggy pouch of skin under its beak that it uses to scoop up fish. Then it drains the water and swallows all the fish. When a chick needs to be fed, the parent brings up a mouthful of fish and lets the baby feed from the pouch. Yummy!

In the first 56 days of its life, the polyphemus moth caterpillar munches 86,000 times its own birth weight in leaves. That's like a human baby eating six large truckloads of food!

The insides of many baby birds' mouths are brightly colored. People think that this encourages the parents to feed the hungry chicks.

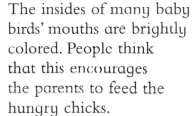

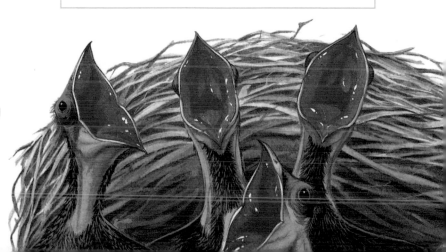

Why do lion cubs chase their mother's tail?

Lion cubs are very playful, and they pounce on anything that moves—especially the tassel on the end of their mom's tail. Games like this teach the cubs how to chase and pounce—skills they'll need when they have to hunt for themselves.

Sea otters know how to have fun. The mother tosses her baby into the air and then catches it.

Playing is how baby animals learn all sorts of important skills for grown-up life.

Why do ducklings play follow-the-leader?

When ducklings hatch, they follow the first moving thing they see, which is usually their mother. By following her everywhere, they learn how to swim and feed. And if they wander off, she just has to call and they fall in line!

Some parents teach their young how to use tools. Baby chimps soon learn how to dig for termites with a stick.

When does a puppy turn into a dog?

Every puppy is blind and helpless when it's born, but by the time it's two years old, it will be fully grown. All pups are about the same size when they're born, whatever type of dog they are. So it takes smaller breeds less time to finish growing up!

2. By six weeks, the puppy is starting to explore. It plays with its brothers and sisters and enjoys tumbling!

LASSIE

1. At about two weeks, the puppy's eyes and ears open. It will soon begin walking.

A baby wildebeest runs before it even walks! The youngster trots along beside its mother just five minutes after it's born.

When does a tiger cub leave home?

A mother tiger takes care of her cubs until they're about two years old. But then she has another litter and ignores the older cubs. It's not actually cruel— the two-year-olds are grown up by then, and it's about time they took care of themselves.

3. By the time it is fully grown, the dog is strong and active. Good food and exercise will help it stay healthy.

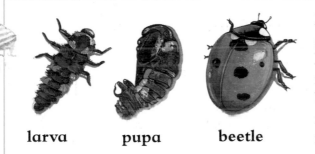

larva   **pupa**   **beetle**

Most insects change shape as they grow. A beetle starts life as a wiggly larva. Then it turns into a pupa. It may not look like it's doing much, but inside the hard skin, the insect is changing fast. When it crawls out, it's a fully grown beetle.

Which baby hides in the forest?

A young deer, called a fawn, is very wobbly on its legs. It couldn't outrun a hungry cougar or wolf. So when it senses danger, the young animal freezes and stays completely still until the danger has passed. The fawn's speckled coat helps it seem almost invisible in the forest's dappled light.

Which babies hide in a circle of horns?

Adult musk oxen make a circle around their calves when danger threatens. They stand close together, with their heads lowered, facing the enemy like a row of shields. It takes a brave and hungry wolf to attack the wall of long, curved horns!

Many animals make noises to scare away enemies. Young burrowing owls, which live in holes in the ground, can make a noise like a rattlesnake when they are threatened.

Which mother pretends she's sick?

If a hungry hunter threatens a plover's nest, the mother bird pretends to be wounded. She flaps a wing as if it is broken and flutters weakly along the ground, moving away from the nest. She wants the enemy to think that she is injured and would be easy to capture. That way, the hunter will go after her, not her babies.

A mother scorpion protects her newborn young by carrying them on her back. If an enemy approaches, she arches her poison-tipped tail high above her back. That usually stops the enemy from coming any closer!

Which baby is always being washed?

A mother cat licks her kittens from the moment they're born. Licking roughly around a newborn kitten's mouth makes it gasp and start breathing. The mother's tongue dries the kitten's fur, too, keeping the kitten warm.

Flamingos preen their chick's feathers as well as their own. They peck out dirt and insects and spread oil over the feathers. This oil is produced by the bird's oil glands and makes the feathers waterproof.

Mud may not seem like a good thing to clean yourself with, but there is nothing a baby hippo likes more than wallowing in a mud bath! Believe it or not, the mud protects the hippo's skin from the sun and keeps it soft.

Who enjoys being groomed?

A baboon makes sure her babies are well groomed. Working slowly, section by section, she parts the fur and picks carefully with her fingers. She removes pieces of dead skin, insects, and dirt—and most of what she finds, she eats!

Sometimes, a foal snaps at its mother, but it's just being friendly! The "biting" action is the foal's way of asking its mother to nuzzle it and groom its coat.

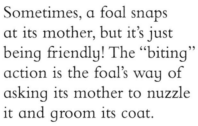

Which baby lives in the cleanest nest?

Many animals keep their babies' nests clean, but the badger would probably win first prize! Adult badgers regularly line their burrows with fresh dried grass and leaves. They even dig special holes far away from their burrow that the whole family uses as toilets.

OCCUPIED

How does a lamb find its mother?

Mother sheep and their lambs sometimes get separated in a crowded field. Most lambs look the same, but each one has its own distinctive call. Every mother sheep knows her own baby's cry and can easily find it in a crowd.

Most whales and dolphins talk to their young and one another by using clicks and other sounds. A baby humpback whale can hear its mom from up to 115 miles (185km) away, so it never gets lost!

A mother moose nudges her baby from behind. This tells the young moose that it has to keep moving, even if it is feeling tired!

Which baby gets spanked when it's naughty?

When a baby elephant is naughty, its mother punishes her calf by hitting it with her trunk. The calf learns quickly what it should and should not do! But a mother elephant also uses her trunk to nuzzle her baby and other young elephants in the herd. This is a sign of affection.

Wolf cubs learn how to howl by copying the sounds their parents make.

The manatee nuzzles her young and cradles it in her flippers to prevent it from floating away in the current.

Index